Walruses

BY KARA L. LAUGHLIN

The Child's World®
childsworld.com

Published by The Child's World®
1980 Lookout Drive • Mankato, MN 56003-1705
800-599-READ • www.childsworld.com

DESIGN ELEMENTS
© creatOR76/Shutterstock.com: porthole
© keren-seg/Shutterstock.com: water

PHOTO CREDITS
© Aleksei Verhovski/Shutterstock.com: 15; Andreea Acaprariter/
Shutterstock.com: 14; DavidBukach/iStockphoto.com: 18; Janelle
Lugge/Shutterstock.com: 19; Sergey Uryadnikov/Shutterstock.
com: 17; tryton2011/Shutterstock.com: cover, 1, 5, 11; Vladimir
Melnik/Shutterstock.com: 6-7, 8-9, 12-13, 20-21

ISBN: 9781503816947
LCCN: 2016945858

Printed in the United States of America
PA02326

NOTE FOR PARENTS AND TEACHERS

The Child's World® helps early readers develop their
informational-reading skills by providing easy-to-read books
that fascinate them and hold their interest. Encourage new
readers by following these simple ideas:

BEFORE READING

- Page briefly through the book. Discuss the photos. What
does the reader think he or she will learn in this book? Let
the child ask questions.
- Look at the glossary together. Discuss the words.

READ THE BOOK

- Now read the book together, or let the child read the book
independently.

AFTER READING

- Urge the child to think more. Ask questions such as, "What
things are different among the animals shown in this book?"

Contents

Two Long Tusks

What if you had two long **tusks**? Would you know how to use them? A walrus would.

Walruses are big animals. They live in the **Arctic Circle**. They live in the water and on land.

Did you know?

A walrus's tusks can be 3 feet (1 meter) long.

Flippers and Whiskers

Walruses have **flippers** and whiskers. These body parts help them in the sea. Flippers help walruses to swim fast. Whiskers help them feel around in the dark water.

Did you know?

The flippers have bumps that help walruses grip the ice.

Tusks and Blubber

Tusks are very long teeth. Walruses poke their tusks into the ice to pull themselves up on land.

Did you know?

Walrus tusks never stop growing.

The sea is cold. **Blubber** is a thick layer of fat. It keeps walruses warm.

Walrus Families

A male walrus is called a **bull**. A female walrus is called a **cow**. Baby walruses are called **calves**.

Walruses live in herds. Bulls live in one herd. Cows and calves live in another.

Did you know?

Calves are born knowing how to swim.

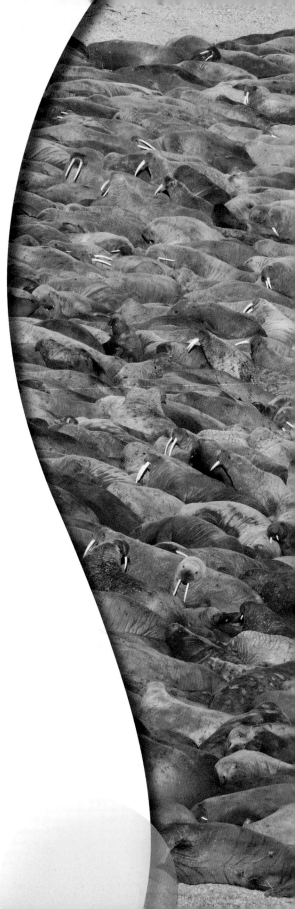

On the Move

Some walruses **migrate**. In winter, they go south. In summer, they go north.

A herd can have hundreds of walruses.

Food

Walruses like to eat clams. They eat sea worms, shrimp, and other things, too. Walruses sometimes eat fish.

Did you know?

Some walruses can eat 3,000 clams in one meal.

Most walrus food is on the sea bottom. The ocean is dark. A walrus uses its whiskers to find food.

Hunted Walruses

Walruses are big. Their skin is tough. Most animals do not eat them. But polar bears and killer whales do.

Did you know?

A walrus can hold its breath for 30 minutes.

People once hunted walruses.
Then there were very few left.

Now walruses are protected. Few people hunt them today.

Walruses look fun and friendly. But they are wild. They are important animals. They are part of a healthy ocean.

Did you know?

Walruses live for about 40 years.

GLOSSARY

Arctic Circle (ARK-tik SIR-kul): The land around the North Pole that stays cold all year is the Arctic Circle. In the Arctic Circle, every year has at least one day when the sun never sets.

blubber (BLUB-bur): The thick fat under a walrus's skin that keeps it warm is called blubber.

bull (BUL): A male walrus is called a bull.

calves (KAVS): Baby walruses are called calves.

cow (KOW): A female walrus is called a cow.

flippers (FLIP-purz): Flippers are webbed limbs that some animals have instead of arms and legs. Flippers help walruses swim in the sea and move on land.

migrate (MY-grayt): When animals migrate, they move as a group from one location to another.

species (SPEE-sheez): A type of a certain animal. There used to be 20 species of walruses. Now there is only one species.

tusk (TUSK): A very long tooth is called a tusk.

TO LEARN MORE

On the Web

Visit our Web page for
lots of links about walruses:
www.childsworld.com/links

Note to parents, teachers, and librarians:
We routinely verify our Web links to make
sure they are safe, active sites—
so encourage your readers
to check them out!

In the Library

Markovics, Joyce L. *My Skin is Gray and Wrinkly.*
New York, NY: Bearport Publishing, 2014.

Owen, Ruth. *Walruses.* New York, NY: Windmill Books, 2013.

Schuetz, Kari. *Walruses.* Minneapolis, MN:
Bellwether Media, 2017.

INDEX

About the Author

Kara L. Laughlin is an artist and writer who lives in Virginia with her husband, three kids, two guinea pigs, and a dog. She is the author of two dozen nonfiction books for kids.